I Got a Pet!

My Pet Snake

By Brienna Rossiter

www.littlebluehousebooks.com

Copyright © 2023 by Little Blue House, Mendota Heights, MN 55120. All rights reserved. No part of this book may be reproduced or utilized in any form or by any means without written permission from the publisher.

Little Blue House is distributed by North Star Editions:
sales@northstareditions.com | 888-417-0195

Produced for Little Blue House by Red Line Editorial.

Photographs ©: Shutterstock Images, cover, 4, 7, 8–9, 11, 12, 15, 17, 20, 22–23, 24 (top left), 24 (top right), 24 (bottom left), 24 (bottom right); iStockphoto, 19

Library of Congress Control Number: 2022901884

ISBN
978-1-64619-593-0 (hardcover)
978-1-64619-620-3 (paperback)
978-1-64619-672-2 (ebook pdf)
978-1-64619-647-0 (hosted ebook)

Printed in the United States of America
Mankato, MN
082022

About the Author

Brienna Rossiter is a writer and editor who lives in Minnesota.

Table of Contents

My Pet Snake **5**

Fun with My Snake **13**

Snake Care **21**

Glossary **24**

Index **24**

My Pet Snake

I have a pet snake.

My snake lives in a tank.

The tank has plants and branches.
My snake can climb on them.

The tank has a water dish. My snake can crawl inside the dish.

The tank has places where my snake can hide. My snake can be hard to see.

Fun with My Snake

The tank has glass sides.

I can watch my snake move around.

Sometimes I take my snake out of its tank.

I pick it up carefully.

That way, I don't scare it.

My snake can sit in my hands.

I hold it gently.

I see its scales up close.

17

My snake can crawl on my shoulder.
It can hang around my neck.

Snake Care

I put a heat lamp on my snake's tank.
The lamp keeps my snake warm.

My snake eats rats

or mice.

I give my snake a mouse.

My snake swallows

it whole.

Glossary

dish

scales

heat lamp

shoulder

Index

C
crawling, 8, 18

E
eating, 22

H
hiding, 10

W
watching, 13